Woman On The Move

*Your Guide to Navigating Through
Life's Transitions*

Tonya McGill

Woman On The Move

Your Guide to Navigating Through Life's Transitions

Tonya McGill

Pen2Pad Ink Publishing

Tonya McGill

Library of Congress Cataloging–In– Publication Data

Name: McGill, Tonya, author.
Title: Woman On The Move / Tonya McGill

Identifiers:
LCCN 2020916287
ISBN 978-1-970135-60-2 (Paperback)
ISBN 978-1-970135-61-9 (Hardcover)
ISBN 978-1-970135-62-6 (Ebook)

Published in the United States by
Pen2Pad Ink Publishing
www.pen2padink.org

Requests to publish work from this book or to contact the author should be sent to:
tonya.mcgill22@gmail.com

Tonya McGill retains the rights to all images.

Tonya McGill

Dedication

This book is dedicated to 3 special people who are no longer with me on earth, but I keep them with me always. They are all at home with Jesus. They raised me and showed me how to keep moving through life no matter what life brought your way.

My maternal grandmother, Gladys Benton, whom I affectionately called "Mama Gladys."

My paternal grandmother, Earnestine Hale Phillips, whom I affectionately called "Maedear".

My daddy, James C. Rhynes, the best dad a girl could ever ask for. You didn't spoil me. You just loved me well.

Thank you all for living a life that inspired me and challenged me to be all God intended for me to be; for encouraging me to never settle and teaching me to love and serve others. I am who I am because of all that each of you poured into me.

To my mom, Bettye B. Rhynes, who is still a big part of my life. I am grateful for the work ethic you instilled in me. As well as your "get it done" mentality that you passed on to me. I keep it moving because of your example!

Table of Contents

Tonya McGill

Foreword

From the very first moment I met Tonya in high school, I knew she was different. Her conversation, her poise, and pleasant personality made me want to get to know her better. The first thing that attracted me to her was her beauty. After speaking with her for a few moments, I realized she was *much* more than a pretty face. There was a tremendous depth to her and an unselfishness that I found to be rare in someone so young. It is no surprise to me that she has blossomed into the beautiful Wife, Mother, Grandmother, Pastor, Leader, and now the Author she is today.

I am so excited that you have decided to make an investment into a better you as she shares her experiences, failures, and successes within the pages of this book. Since we started in ministry together 21 years ago, she has had an undying passion to encourage, uplift, and position women to embrace their purpose and God-given destinies. Her candid transparency and warm approach will make it easy to turn these pages and start blossoming into the woman God created you to be. I have watched her in countless conferences, leadership meetings, and panel discussions designed to launch people forward. She's the real deal. She is gifted in so many areas and provides a deeply personal, relatable, and easy to understand approach. She truly loves what she does and delivers with a passion and a spirit of excellence.

She is a woman who is really for women and I can assure you that you won't find a better champion than Tonya. I am so blessed to be married to such a strong woman and life partner who has walked by my side since that first conversation. What you will read in these pages is truly sincere and authentic. I have lived with the author through every season that life has thrown our way. I pray that you will grow and be encouraged after reading the first of many books she will author. Enjoy "Woman on the Move."

Norris Q. McGill
Senior Pastor
Antioch Christian Church

Preface

The journey of a woman's life can be filled with twists and turns as she goes through different phases of her life. There is no escaping it. Life is constantly moving, and we must learn how to move with it. Whether single or married, with or without children, in school or pursuing business, or the life of the party or in a season of loneliness, we can seize the moment or allow the moment to be wasted.

Ecclesiastes 3:1 (The Message) states that "There's an opportune time to do things, a right time for everything on the earth." I believe every moment of our life is orchestrated by the Lord. In these moments, we must focus on listening and hearing His voice. We need to simply obey when He is speaking. A key element to success for those of us in transition is to think correctly.

Someone once said, "Just when I think I have learned the way to live, life changes." The truth in that statement speaks volumes. Most of us decided when we were young what our lives would look like as a teen, in college, as a young adult, and as a mature adult. When it doesn't go as planned, we must learn how to pivot and adjust. Otherwise, we end up lost and angry.

I know you have so many aspirations and goals. I hope that this book helps you to understand key points and ideas to help you reach them. I do not have the answer to every question as a woman, but I do have experience. I have a thirst for loving others. I have the drive to help others as I have been helped to move forward. Let us be women on the move together.

Chapter One

Success Begins in the Mind

"For as he thinks within himself, so is he..."
Proverbs 23:7 (TLV)

As the oldest daughter of two lifelong educators, I grew up thinking the key to my success began with a great education. Both my parents were college graduates with degrees in Education. They received their bachelor's degrees and their master's Plus 30 receiving their postgraduate degrees. They both retired from teaching high school after 33 years. They required educational excellence from my sister and me which included good grades throughout our elementary, junior high, and high school years. They also required us to pursue our college degrees as well. I attended college on an academic scholarship and graduated with magna cum laude honors in 4 years. I had my great education. Now, I was ready to live my great life.

My belief was a great education would then lead me to a great profession. A great profession would then lead me to a great income. A great income would then lead me to a great life. After receiving a great education, a great profession, a great income, I fell short of the great I was searching for. It was not until years later as I developed my relationship with the Lord I found out the real key to a great life did not begin with my great education. Rather, it started with a great **thought** life.

There is a quote I love:

*"Watch your thoughts, for they become words.
Watch your words, for they become actions.
Watch your actions, for they become habits.
Watch your habits, for they become character.
Watch your character, for it becomes your destiny."*

Our destinies begin with our thoughts. We live in a world where many people are heavily influenced by the opinions of other people. Social media has changed our world and influenced our relationships with others. It has even influenced our evaluation of ourselves. We often compare ourselves to the people we are connected to on social media and even how many likes/comments we receive on our posts. This standard can be especially harmful and challenging for the Believer, those who are followers of Christ. The standard for Believers must be the Word of God.

Romans 12:2 (TPT) recommends that we *"Stop imitating the ideals and opinions of the culture around you but be inwardly transformed by the Holy Spirit through a total reformation on how you think. This will empower you to discern God's will as you live a beautiful life, satisfying and perfect in his eyes."* Shift your thought to be what God wants instead of people of the world.

Is this easy? Of course not! It is hard to do what this scripture is telling us because we live in the world. We are surrounded by pop culture, influenced by social media, and bombarded with what the world says we should be. Yet, Believers are given a different measurement. Believers are encouraged to be different than those around them; to be *uncommon*, not *common*. To be *uncommon* means "to be unusual, abnormal, rare, unexpected, and atypical."

So much of our success comes down to our minds. If we are going to change our ways, we must begin by changing our thoughts. We become new by developing a new mindset. With our minds, we can BE what the Word declares we are and experience good success. The new mindset we develop should be created based upon who we were created to be. It should not be who others define us to be.

Success versus Good Success

The one word that probably describes the so-called "American Dream" would be the word *success*. Everybody wants to succeed. They want to be associated with success. We even look at a successful post as one with the most likes or views on social media. I had my own definitions of success growing up and pursued those. For example, I didn't want to be a teacher because I didn't think it would pay enough and give me the options to buy things I thought would make me successful.

Joshua 1:8 (NKJV) states, *"This Book of the Law shall not depart from your mouth, but you shall meditate in it day and night, that you may observe to do according to all that is written in it. For then you will make your way prosperous, and then you will have good success."*

We women on the move should not be content to just have *success*. The goal should be *good success*. That is the success that brings peace and fulfillment no matter what is going on around you, no matter what season you are in, no matter how much money you have, and no matter how many likes you get on Instagram. This success is what we should strive for to consistently navigate through life's transitions.

In Joshua 1:8, the Word of God states we will find *good success* when we keep our minds focused upon the truth of who we are and who we were created to be, which is in the Word of God. For a woman on the move, *good success* is not about popularity, power, prestige, or position. *Good success* is not about choosing your own path with your own goals. *Good success* is about following the path God has created for you before the foundation of the earth. It is about walking in alignment with His purpose and His will for your life. *Good success* is about meditating on God's Word and renewing your mind with the Word, so you do what the Word declares. *Good success* is about thinking in alignment with God's perspective and not your own perspective or the world.

Good success in God's kingdom differs from the world standard of success. Here are some examples of differences. The names are fake, but the situations are real.

World View (Success)	Kingdom View (Good Success)
Materialistic Growth and Gain	***Spiritual Growth and Gain***
Shirley is a successful singer that can afford all the cars and houses she likes. However, she has no one to share her success with.	Taylor is a wealthy banker that makes time for time with the Lord, her family, and friends she loves.
Jack of All Trades	***Faithfulness***
Melissa is a mom, an award-winning artist, and she runs her own painting company. While she has a successful painting company, she is also opening a restaurant and beauty salon.	Draya is a mom who works as a professor at a college, works at home as a mom, and has been married for over 20 years. She falters sometimes at doing one of her jobs, but she never lets it keep her from knowing her priorities.
Self-First	***Others First***
Mary buys herself more shoes, knowing her son has shoes with holes in them.	Jessica makes sure her daughters have clothes and food even though she is a single mom who does not receive financial support from her ex-husband.

Faith in Self

Minnie puts enormous pressure on herself to become a partner in her law firm. She works 7 days a week and never takes vacation.

Faith in God

Laila is passed for a promotion at her supermarket job. Instead of getting angry, she continues to be an immaculate manager in the produce department. Six months later, she becomes general manager for the supermarket.

Pride

Diana does not want to admit she needs help reading the contract she has received to become a professional model.

Boldness

Ursula asks for help understanding key terms and definitions at her new job as a Security Supervisor.

God's Word is essential to Christian success. It does not mean we will not have a life without problems, but it means that we can overcome every obstacle because the Word of God is powerful. The Word of God is the only truth we can depend on and live by to obtain true success. A prerequisite for obtaining this success during transition is a woman who has her mind changed.

My mind was trained to be intellectual, to process things that made sense. I took great pride in studying in class and in understanding the principles being taught in my classes. I was and still am a person who loves to learn. I love researching. I love analyzing, and I love seeking best practices. Nothing is wrong with any of these habits; however, sometimes, you will be forced to grow through a season by changing habits.

My mind certainly had to change. I found myself doing what I avoided - teaching as my father, mother and sister even though my classroom was in church. The journey from corporate America to ministry was filled with excitement, passion, and purpose. The journey also included moments of uncertainty, discomfort, and even fear. If my mind was not changed, I certainly would not have made it through one of the most challenging yet rewarding seasons of my life.

Meditation:

"Life is not measured by the number of breaths we take, but by the moments that take our breath away."

~ Maya Angelou

Reflection Questions:

1. What does "good success" look like to you?

_____

_____

_____

_____

2. What obstacles will you probably have to face trying to achieve "good success"?

_____

_____

_____

_____

3. Who can support you on your journey to good success? How can they help you?

_____

_____

_____

_____

Chapter Two

Shifting Into Gear

"Neither do people pour new wine into old wineskins. If they do, the skins will burst; the wine will run out and the wineskins will be ruined. No, they pour new wine into new wineskins, and both are preserved." Matthew 9: 17

There is a song we used to sing in my church growing up, part of the lyrics said "I looked at my hands, my hands looked new. I looked at my feet and they did too." This sounds good, but it is not the truth. After we give our lives to Jesus, the only thing that changes is our spirit man; we are now renewed in our spirit so we have fellowship with the Father. Our bodies and minds are not changed. A woman on the move must know that for her life to shift her mind must shift.

To have a different mindset, we must do the work by exchanging the thoughts we had before Jesus with receiving new thoughts built upon the Word of God. We build a new mindset by RENEWING our minds. The way we think must be totally reformed. We cannot lay new thoughts on top of our old thoughts; we must replace new thoughts for the old ones. This is not a one-time-only thing. It is a daily grind. It is a daily evaluation. It is a daily pursuit. It is developing a new mindset based upon the Word of God and His will for you.

Work goes into developing a new mindset. It requires the discipline of the mind and the body. It is tearing down mindsets you may have had for years. It is meditating day and night on new thoughts. We will want to take the easy road and stick with what the world thinks. When we do this, we may be moving but not going anywhere. The goal is to move through life's transitions with purpose and power which comes from the Lord.

When our mind is not renewed and we are Believers, we can have the right God but not the right mentality. We see this in scripture in Numbers 13. In this chapter, God instructed Moses to send men to scout out the land He was giving to His children as He delivered them from Egypt. God has taken them out of slavery and leading them into a land He promised He would give them. Moses chose and commissioned leaders to go first into the land and bring back an in-person account of what God had prepared for them. The way the leaders thought about what they saw caused them to miss what God had prepared for them. Instead of aligning their thinking with what God said, they disagreed and died in the wilderness. God said "It's yours." They said, "We aren't able."

Numbers 13:31 states *But the men who had gone up with him said, "We are not able to go up against the people, for they are stronger than we."* Their confession spread to others in the congregation and brought great distress to many. The way the leaders thought infected the way the others thought. They were on the move but went nowhere because of their thinking. They were no longer bound in Egypt; however, they were still bound in their minds.

The way we think can bind us more than any chains. Ignorance and error of God and His ways bind us more than any chains. We can be living well in the promise land or wandering aimlessly in the wilderness.

For example, a person who may be in jail can, with knowledge of the Word, continue to have peace and joy just by knowing God's

Word. Likewise, people who are free can feel like they are trapped because they have no joy or peace operating out of self. God's Word is full of promises for us as believers. Nonetheless, we don't see ourselves as having those promises because we are not in an agreement with the Word, and we have not renewed our minds with the Word.

When our minds are renewed, we will do things that are *uncommon*; things that are different from the world. Renewed thinking will produce uncommon works. God desires to take us to a new level; however, we must get into agreement with His plan for us. If it is not in line with the Word, then we do not need to think on these things.

The Children of Israel's minds were not renewed – their thinking had not changed from their time in bondage to their freedom. They placed more emphasis on what they saw instead of what God said to them. They rejected the Word of God. Nothing changes in our lives until our thinking changes. I can miss my blessing by not thinking in line with the Word of God, by looking at how I see things rather than what God said.

The mind is where spiritual battles are won or lost. Our victory is obtained through our thinking. With our minds, we take possession of what Jesus has done for us. This makes the mind such a battlefield for the enemy.

We can control our thoughts and make them line up with God's Word. We do not have to allow Satan to defeat us through a defeated mentality. We must take every thought captive and *make* it line up with the Word of God. This requires discipline by thinking about what we think about. This is more than positive thinking; this is Godly thinking.

Renewed thinking requires grit and guts. We cannot be a people pleaser and think like everyone else thinks. We must be a God pleaser. It takes grit, guts, and courage to not focus on what people say and please God. To have a renewed mindset, we must rely on God more than ourselves. We must not give up, give out, or give in. We must determine to walk by faith and not by sight. We must set our affection on things above. We must count it all joy.

Renewed thinking is doing, seeing, and responding to life differently. *Renewed thinking* means we are just different; we don't see a hopeless situation. He has filled us with hope and we don't abandon our assignment when it gets hard because we know His grace is sufficient for us. We don't back up or shrink back. We press forward.

Meditation:

"We are what we repeatedly do. Excellence, then, is not an act, but a habit."

~Aristotle

Reflection Question:

1. How do you see yourself?

_____

_____

_____

_____

2. Does it matter more to you what others think, what you think, or what the Word of God says? Why?

_____

_____

_____

_____

3. What are some old habits you need to change?

_____

_____

_____

_____

Chapter Three

Moving Despite Loss

"I have told you these things, so that in me you may have [perfect] peace. In the world you have tribulation and distress and suffering, but be courageous [be confident, be undaunted, be filled with joy]; I have overcome the world." [My conquest is accomplished, my victory abiding].
John 16:33 (Amplified)

Eve was the first woman and the mother of all living. Eve was created as an answer to a problem. In Genesis 2:18, the Word says, *"And the Lord God said, "It is not good that man should be alone; I will make him a helper comparable to him."* God said that Adam needed someone who could be his equal. His partner. Someone that he could experience life with. Eve came on the scene perfect. I believe she had the perfect body, the perfect relationship with her husband, and the perfect relationship with God. All was perfect until it wasn't.

Eve had everything initially, but then she experienced a tremendous loss because of her disobeying the voice of God and listening to the voice of the enemy. Her transition through life then became riddled with blame, disappointment, loss of fellowship with her husband, and even the loss of a child. Eve's worst loss was loss of fellowship with God.

As we move through life, loss will happen along the journey. Some of the losses will bring disappointment. Some will bring discouragement. Some will bring distress. However, as women on the move, we can go through this transition with peace.

One of the most challenging losses I experienced came on April 5, 2005, with the passing of my daddy. If there was a poster child for a "Daddy's Girl", my face would be front and center. I have always been and will always be a "Daddy's Girl". My dad, James C. Rhynes, was the best father any girl could ask for. He treated my sister and I like princesses. He often told people we were not spoiled. Instead, we were just well-loved. He taught us so much about life, how to deal with people, how to understand free enterprise (nothing is free), how to work hard, and how to love well.

One fear I always expressed was that I

don't know how I will make it if my dad passes away. My daddy was diagnosed in March 2005 with lung cancer and passed away in April 2005. He was in Shreveport, Louisiana in the hospital while my sister and I were in Dallas, Texas. For a month, we spent many hours on I-20 and in the air going back and forth to check on him. During this time, I was still a wife, mom of 3 children, and First Lady of a growing church. I was amazed how I kept moving. But I know it was truly because of the Grace of God.

I will never forget the one night I was in the Emergency room with my dad. The doctors told us he may not make it through the night. When the doctors left, it was just my dad and me. I asked him was he afraid. My daddy boldly proclaimed, "I am not afraid, Tonya. I know Jesus is my Lord and Savior and I will be with Him whenever I die. I wish I had more time with you, your sister and to see my grandchildren grow up. But I am not afraid." I was so filled with peace and sadness all at the same time.

My dad did not pass away that night. He passed 3 weeks later, and I was standing by his bedside as he transitioned to heaven. Through my tears and grief, I remembered his words. The best gift I received in this moment of loss was, before my dad took his last breath, he turned his head and looked at me, closed his eyes, and went to be with Jesus. I will never forget that moment. The loss has been great, yet my heart is encouraged. I know the loss is temporary because I believe we will be together again when the Lord returns OR when I go to be with them.

Your story of loss may not be the loss of a loved one. It may be the loss of a job or the loss of a friendship. Loss hurts. Loss brings pain. Loss brings tears. But joy also comes in the morning as it says in Psalm 30:5. Even though you may experience loss during transition, keep moving you will get through and get to the other side of loss if you don't quit.

Meditation:

"The experience of pain or loss can be a formidably motivating force."

~ John C. Maxwell

Reflection Questions:

1. What is the most painful loss you have experienced thus far in your life?

_____

_____

_____

_____

2. Is there any brokenness in your life that's keeping you from moving forward?

_____

_____

_____

_____

3. What encouragement would you give to someone else who is experiencing loss in their life?

_____

_____

_____

_____

Chapter Four

Being Still Yet Moving

Do not be anxious about anything, but in everything by prayer and supplication with thanksgiving let your requests be made known to God. Philippians 4:6

Sarah (originally named Sarai) was the wife of Abraham. Sarai was a beautiful woman, but she could not have children. It was expected during this time that wives bear a son, so their husband's name would continue. God appeared to Abraham when he was 99 years old and made a covenant with him. God told Abraham he would be the father of many nations. His descendants more numerous than the stars in the sky. He also spoke about Sarah in Genesis 17: 15-16 (NIV):

"God also said to Abraham, "As for Sarai your wife, you are no longer to call her Sarai; her name will be Sarah. I will bless her and will surely give you a son by her. I will bless her so that she will be the mother of nations; kings of peoples will come

from her."

After many years of waiting, Sarah became impatient. She convinced her husband to have sex with her handmaiden, Hagar, to produce a child. A child, Ishmael, was born to Hagar and Abraham, but this was not the child God told Sarah that Abraham would have. God specifically said Sarah would bear the child, not Hagar. Sarah's impatience led her to make a rash decision.

I am so thankful God honors His Word. At 90, Sarah received what God promised her – she bore a son named Isaac. (Genesis 21:1) Despite Sarah's impatience, God kept His promise. Sarah found out that, even though she was impatient, God remained faithful to what He promised her.

My husband and I have this joke between us. He told me one time, "If you were God, you would not have waited 6 days to create the earth, and you would have created it in one day."

My response to him was, "If you were God, you would still be thinking about what you were going to make."

That is such a real example of the type of personalities he and I have. He's the one who takes his time to think carefully about what he will do and I think and move in one swoop.

As you can tell, I've struggled with patience. I probably have given birth to many Ishmael's in my own life because of my impatience to wait for the perfect gift God promised me. Many of us can relate to Sarah. We look around and see what others have and want ours too. We grow tired of waiting. We get uncomfortable waiting. We doubt waiting. We feel compelled to act immediately.

I know the word "wait" is a four-letter word. It's a short word and powerful word. It is also a difficult word to put into action because we want to know the unknown. However, think of what can happen if you choose to experience what God wants you to experience. His wealth and love are bigger than anything we can even imagine! No need to be the hare. With God, take your time and be the tortoise.

Meditation:

"Patience is not simply the ability to wait - it's how we behave while we're waiting."

~ Joyce Meyer

Reflection Questions:

1. What part of your life do you think you are the most impatient with? Why?

_____

_____

_____

_____

2. How can you occupy your time so you can be patient for what you need?

_____

_____

_____

_____

3. Who or what can help you to develop patience?

_____

_____

_____

_____

Chapter Five

It's Ok To Not Be Ok

I have said these things to you, that in me you may have peace. In the world you will have tribulation. But take heart; I have overcome the world."
(John 16:33 ESV)

Transitions can be exciting, but they can also bring apprehension. At times we may feel as though there is something wrong with us or our faith if we don't feel ok while going through transitions.

"Everything will be okay in the end, if it's not okay it's not the end." – John Lennon

I've discussed the miracle God gave Sarah and Abraham despite Sarah's impatience, but how did Hagar fare in this situation? Hagar minded her own business. She was a slave, and she had accepted that. As a slave, she had no right to say no.

So, when Sarah comes knocking at her

door and said, "What are you doing? Stop ironing my clothes, stop cleaning up, and be with my husband."

I can imagine that Hagar's mouth dropped and said, "Do what now?" Sarah continued. "What's about to happen is Abraham is going to come in and sleep with you. Then, I hope you get pregnant quick so the baby can come and you can give the baby to me."

Hagar was obedient to her master, Sarah. She and Abraham did what you do to have babies, and she became pregnant. Then, something shifted in Hagar. I believe she started "feeling herself" for the first time. She felt like she was better than Sarah. She felt like she could do something her owner could not. In Hagar's mind, she probably thought *she needs me. At some point, she will take my baby... but for the next 9 months, she has to care for me.*

Sarah was mad and she tried to take it out on Abraham. He said, "Nope. You deal with her." Now Sarah had to put Hagar in check. Sarah deals with Hagar so harshly that Hagar leaves. Hagar was running away from an unpleasant situation with Sarah. Even though Hagar is a slave for Sarah, Hagar will not stay where she does not feel safe.

There are some things we can learn from not being ok. We can run, but we cannot hide. Hagar learned the same lesson. She ran away from Sarah and Abraham. In my opinion, she was also running away from God because of her experiences with Him while living in Abraham and Sarah's household. When she ended up in the wilderness near her hometown of Shur, she talked to God personally. The talk changed her life. God didn't speak to her when she was pretty and put together. He helped her when she was her most desperate and NOT ok.

When I was a new Christian, I would always feel intimidated to share the realness of my life. I would spend time with women who went on and on about their hours of prayer time, their multiple Bible Study groups, and their numerous Sunday worship services. The reality of my life was that I was a wife, mom of 3 active young children, and I worked full time outside the home. If I was going to spend an hour in prayer, I would have to wake up by 4 am every morning because my day usually began 5:30 am with waking everyone up, getting everyone dressed, fed and in the car by 7:15 am so I could do drop offs and make it to work myself by 8:30 am. Honestly, I did not have the physical strength to wake up that time every day. I felt ashamed to say to those ladies I still love God without praying for hours. I wanted someone to say: It's ok to not be ok.

A great scripture I found that encouraged me to be ok not being ok is in *2 Corinthians 12: 9-10:*

"But he replied, "My gift of undeserved grace is all you need. My power is strongest when you are weak." So if Christ keeps giving me this power, I will gladly brag about how weak I am. [10] Yes, I am glad to be weak or insulted or mistreated or to have troubles and sufferings, for it is for Christ. Because when I am weak, I am strong."

We have been taught that we must always have it all together. We must be perfection walking. When perfection does not show up in our lives, we become disappointed. We have expectations that, to be a strong, confident woman, we must have no weaknesses. Weakness means something is wrong, and we refuse to acknowledge that we are not okay because we fear being judged, ridiculed, or labeled as a weak woman.

Our expectation is that a strong, confident BOSS woman is a woman who has all the answers all the time. She not only has all the answers, but she has her emotions always under control. She is always smiling. She is always dressed immaculately. She is always sharing a great news report about her business, her husband, her children, and her life. She is a volunteer with her children's organizations. She is the "room mom" of the Kindergarten class. She serves in her church. She cooks home-cooked meals for her family and always gives great news reports about her family, her finances, her friendships, and her faith. Girl, that is exhausting!

Strength requires none of those attributes or characteristics. Strength is admitting you have weaknesses. Strength means admitting that you are a work in progress. Strength is knowing that your children or your husband have faults, but those faults do not outweigh their greatness. In this journey called life – the highs and lows of motherhood or whatever role you're playing- there will be days when you are ok and days when you are not. That is ok.

In the midst of every struggle, there is an opportunity for us grow deeper in our faith as we learn more about the Lord. We can also learn more about ourselves, embrace the moment and the season we are in now. This allows our hearts to be healed, our minds to be renewed, and our vision to be clearer for where God is taking us.

It's ok to not be ok. Why? Because the Word says when I am weak, then I am strong. Think of this - When I am strong on my own, then I am weak because I am on my own; my power is limited. His power is unlimited. On my own, I have limits. With Him, there are no limits.

The reflection questions in this section are based on how I coped when I wasn't ok. Hopefully, you will find your routine or niche that will help you in these moments.

Meditation:

"Your joy comes from how you think, the choices that we make in life."

~ Joyce Meyer

Reflection Questions:

1. What can you do that can help you stop, be quiet, and listen?

_____

_____

_____

_____

2. What can you do that will help you be more emotionally stable?

_____

_____

_____

_____

3. What Bible verse or quote can help you remember courage and confidence when you are feeling not ok?

_____

_____

_____

_____

Chapter Six

Keep it Moving

"Not that I have already obtained this or am already perfect, but I press on to make it my own, because Christ Jesus has made me his own. Brothers, I do not consider that I have made it my own. But one thing I do: forgetting what lies behind and straining forward to what lies ahead, I press on toward the goal for the prize of the upward call of God in Christ Jesus." Philippians 3:12-14

"It's just too hard."

"I can't do it anymore."

"Why is this happening to me?"

"When will I ever get IT together?"

Have you made these statements or asked these questions? I certainly have throughout my life journey. There have been times when I did not think I had the strength to keep moving.

"Courage is not having the strength to go on; it is going on when you don't have the strength."
Theodore Roosevelt

Sometimes, we do not understand the proper relationship we should have with the Lord. We are to be partners with Him through active participation. We can't just sit back, expecting God to do everything for me. He helps us. He does not do it for us. He has a part, but we also have a part. We must believe, we speak, and have works to go along with our faith.

When we read about women in the Bible, we can be encouraged they were not perfect. Neither are we. We are continuous works of improvement. The only way that improvement can happen, however, is if we keep looking forward even when it seems really hard. Consider the story of Lot with the cities of Sodom and Gomorrah. (Genesis 19) Angels came to him with his family to let him know that they intended to destroy everything. EVERYTHING! Now, if angels came to me and told me what they were going to do, I would immediately listen and pretty much do whatever they told me. Lot's wife, however, needed a little more convincing. When it was time for the family to flee, she looked back at the destruction. When she did, God turned her into a pillar of salt. Ouch.

When I partner with the Lord, I keep my eyes upon Him and not the things that come to distract me. When we keep our eyes on Jesus, we look forward, not behind. To move forward into the new, we must forget the former things. We cannot dwell on the past. Dwelling on the past will not change it. The enemy used to deceive me into thinking if I could just figure out the why of my past mistakes, then, I will not repeat the same mistakes.

My focus became searching for the why rather than focusing on the Lord, and that brought me only into further bondage and regret. He has to become the center of my life, the center of my focus. When we seek Him first, He will add everything we need (*Matthew 6:33*).

Looking behind will not keep you moving forward. God talks to you about your future and your present. The enemy talks to you about your past. You cannot look at past failures and allow that to paralyze you. Fix your eyes and your gaze upon Jesus. Lot's wife died because she did not look forward but looked behind. We may not die a natural death, but we become stagnant not actively moving in life.

So how do we "keep it moving"? People say that a lot, but it is hard to do if you don't know what steps to take.

Here are some possible ways you can start.

1. **Go somewhere you have never gone before. Don't worry.** You are not by yourself when traveling with Jesus. He's a good friend who will never leave you alone. While it may be unfamiliar to you, it is not to HIM since he knows all.

2. **Value every day.** I realized so many days that instead of waking up dreading my life, I should have been grateful. Every day. Every single day is truly a gift from the Lord. Yes, my day may be filled with crying children, demanding meetings, and lengthy conversations. But it is a gift. Life is precious and short. It is a gift you should focus on what you can do and not what you cannot do.

3. **Consider a new perspective**. The terms *fact* and *truth* appear to have the same meaning, but they do not. *Fact* is the current state. *Truth* is what the Word declares. For example, it is a *fact* that I may be unmarried and without a partner in the natural. The *truth*, however, is that Jesus is always with me, so I am never

really alone or without someone. *Truth* requires you to see yourself how God sees you, and His perspective of you is that you are amazing...flaws and all! When you change your perspective, you understand there is a way out of the wilderness. All is possible. You have purpose. You mean something to this world.

4. **Write goals or visions.** Habakkuk 2 declares to *"...Write the vision; make it plain on tablets, so he may run who reads it."* Proverbs 29:18 states that *"Where there is no prophetic vision the people cast off restraint..."* Goals and visions help us know the direction we are going. Many people think that creating goals and visions is unspiritual because "it shows a lack of trust in God" and "God can't lead when we plan." Yes, God does not want us moving forward without Him, BUT we need to seek HIM for direction. Write goals and visions with HIM. Then, go to work. Remember, we must act as well as listen.

Meditation:

"Our hero status is not dependent on our human might or power or even our human spirit; it comes from the power of His spirit."

~ Lisa Bevere

Reflection Questions:

1. When you were small, what did you see yourself doing when you grew up?

_____

_____

_____

_____

2. Are you currently pursuing your childhood dream? Why or why not?

_____

_____

_____

_____

3. Is it easy for you to see beyond the facts? Why or why not?

_____

_____

_____

_____

Chapter Seven

Tapping Into My Destiny

For I know the plans I have for you, declares the Lord, plans for welfare and not for evil, to give you a future and a hope. Jeremiah 29: 11 (ESV)

Destiny (Noun):

- As what happens in the future: the things that someone or something will experience in the future

- A power believed to control what happens in the future

Many people find themselves in a state of frenzy, fear, and frustration as they seek their destiny or purpose. I used to be that way. I would ask "what am I supposed to do? Am I doing this right?" I think I became so obsessed with getting it right that I got it wrong. Two scriptures helped me gain a different perspective:

Psalm 139:16 NLT, *"You saw me before I was born. Every day of my life was recorded in your book. Every moment was laid out before a single day had passed."*

Ephesians 2:10 *"For we are His workmanship, created in Christ Jesus for good works, which God prepared beforehand that we should walk in them."*

Both scriptures show we can take comfort in the fact that God created us *on purpose, with purpose,* and *for purpose.* Every purpose also has a time. The time you are living in now is your time. Sometimes, it is easy to be positive about our lives when things are going well. During these times, we believe that we have purpose. However, how do we feel when we are in the valley? Did you know there is purpose for your valley? You still have purpose when going through your valley. Everything has a season and a purpose under the heaven. God allows everything to work together for our good. Why? Because He knows the end.

The Lord wants us to find joy in our current state and appreciate the time we're in. We cannot just be excited about our season of receiving if we are not excited about our season of giving. Paul says something very important in the book of Philippians. He said that he learned to be content regardless if he had a lot or nothing (Philippians 4:12) How did Paul learn to be content in different situations? The next verse (4:13) explains that he does it all through Christ who strengthens him.

"Your life isn't an accident. You have a destiny, one that only you can complete." Rick Warren

We must not allow our minds or our bodies to convince us we can only be joyful when things are good. Joy is a choice. There is a time for everything, and I must learn how to experience joy at every time. We can be robbed from experiencing joy in the time we are in because we are waiting for a different time. What is our response in our time? Can we be content? Find joy? Or do we complain? Find fault?

There are 3 hindrances to our tapping into our destiny: *comparison, unhealed wounds,* and *impatience.*

Comparison

Theodore Roosevelt said, "Comparison is the thief of joy." When we compare, some ugly things happen. Comparison opens the door for pride in our lives. When we compare ourselves, we often think we are better than other people, which makes us puffed up OR we get depressed because we think we are less than others. Comparison brings the focus onto us instead of God. Comparison also can make us bitter or resentful of others and what they have if we feel insecure about what we have.

One reason we compare ourselves is that we are insecure. We are insecure about who we are and/or what we have compared to other people. The root of insecurity is fear we lack or fear we are not good enough. Do you know who created you? Do you know who sent you into the earth? Do you know who equipped you? Why would you ever allow the enemy to deceive you into thinking you lack something? To overcome comparison, we must be courageous not afraid. We must be willing to move in confidence and do something we've never done. Step outside of our comfort zone.

Unhealed Wounds

Women, we love hard. We are all in. Sometimes, unfortunately, that exposes us to some hurt. Imperfect people do imperfect things. We must press into the Lord and allow Him to heal us. You will never be healed if you delay honesty with God. Acknowledge the pain, take it to the cross, give it to the

Lord, receive His Word (Don't doubt the Word) and move forward.

We must be healed and healthy! Working out is not something I enjoy, but I want to be healthy. A girl's got to do what a girl's got to do. Yes, it is painful, aggravating, depressing, and a lot of other words associated with pain. But Jesus came to set the captives free, to give us life, and life more abundantly. We must receive our healing, so the wounds can properly heal.

Impatience

Impatience can lead to discouragement which then leads to doubt and unbelief. I believe that, in our human mind, we forget who God is. He is the greater and we are the lesser. We must be persuaded that God knows what He's doing in our lives. This especially happens when we think that Jesus is not moving fast enough or doing what we think He should be doing. We look for another job, another husband, another church, another ministry, another, another, and another. He has already provided for us. He is the truth, the way, and the life. If we do not grow weary, we will receive what we are seeking.

Hannah, another woman from the Bible, (1

Samuel 1) had some problems. She was a part of the original "Desperate Housewives" saga filled with lots of drama. She had a lot of problems: her womb was closed by the Lord, and she had to deal with this woman in her face constantly talking noise. She was so hurt she could not even eat.

If I may show my age for a minute... Remember the "A Different World" episode where Whitley Gilbert went to the therapist because she was so stressed out that her ex-boyfriend, Julian, had moved on to a beautiful woman named Shelby. Her therapist got tired of listening to her whine and whine. So, she gave her some advice I want to give to you today about tapping into your Destiny – "Relax, Relate, and Release!"

Now...back to destiny and our bible character, Hannah...

1. RELAX!

Sometimes, we feel pressure to be and do what others expect rather than what God wants. We allow insecurity to drive us to making rash decisions. Sometimes, we just must to be still, exhale the anxiety, and then breathe in the Lord. When we relax, we can embrace our situation. I must see the blessing in what I have and where I am. This will cause us to change our attitude and our mindset. The best way to relax is just be real. Embrace it. This is where I am. This is what I am dealing with. This is the reality of my situation. You can't ignore it or speak it away. You must deal with it with honesty and truthfulness. Remember I told you Hannah couldn't eat? Eventually, she did. It was her way of relaxing to understand her situation and WHO could help her with it.

2. RELATE!

Your mind AND your emotions can play tricks on you. Believe me, I have experienced it. My feelings do not always reflect God's feelings towards me. I must expect something good like it says in Psalm 27:13: *"I would have lost heart unless I had believed that I would see the goodness of the Lord in the land of the living. [14] wait on the Lord; be of good courage, and He shall strengthen your heart."*

Expectation is a strong belief that something good will happen; it is joyful anticipation. Waiting is not passive. Wait, hope, and work in faith. I am waiting on some things to manifest, but I will not stop sowing, praying, believing, confessing. I believe I will see the good thing God promised me. Hannah wasn't expecting any good. She went year by year with her husband and her nemesis to the temple. But in prayer she got a release. Then, she received a blessing from the prophet, which was like receiving a prophetic word. Hannah had to accept what God wanted her to have not what she wanted.

3. RELEASE!

We must release to receive. You cannot receive anything if you are full of other stuff. LET. IT. GO. Past actions. Past hurts. Past sins. Past emotions. We hold a lot of deep hurts from the past. Maybe we have forgiven, but we have not released. God made me realize that I would say "I forgive," but I didn't release. I held the hurt. I held the "I don't understand." In my mind, I wanted to figure out WHY they did this. I kept saying, "If I could just understand why then I would be okay." It is the significance we attach to the offense that causes the pain. Release it all so your past will not hold back who you will become. You are a Daughter of the King. You are a woman of faith. You are an overcomer.

Hannah decided this thing must end. When she was praying, the priest thought she was drunk (loud, talkative, slurred speech, etc.) Did she care? Not at all! She poured out, and it was God's responsibility to fill her up. The same goes for us. You don't have to allow what's happening around you to happen in you. Fight for your joy. Fight for your good attitude. Fight for your peace!

Think about it. Do you need a "Hannah" moment with the Lord? Do you need PEACE amid your BROKEN PIECES? If so, pour it all out so you can receive what He has for you. Hannah went from receiving a sacrifice from her husband to taking her own. Her relationship with the Lord matured. She made room in her heart for Him by getting rid of all that was there – bitterness, anger, frustration, irritation, sadness, etc. She had to really get real with the Lord. I honestly believe she did the "ugly cry" (runny nose, loud crying, and running eye makeup).

It's time. Get real with the Father. Give Him all that you have been holding on to. Surrender EVERYTHING and expect nothing. Cleanse your heart, cleanse your soul, and allow Him to restore your soul. A sacrifice is about you really giving up that thing that is precious to you so God can give you what you really need. You need to trust He knows what He's doing. Then, remember He wants what's best for you and then release it to Him: your fears, your expectations and desires. When

Hannah said, "If you give me a son, I will give him back," she was at the point of "I want what you want God more than for myself. "

There is a light within you. It burns so that you can shine for the Lord. The creativity that you have, the way that you dress, and the things you like are all part of your creativity. When we deny who we are or change who we are to be like someone else, we end up putting out the light. We cover it and the light eventually diminishes because other things are smothering us. What I hope is that you will let your light shine by being you and doing you. Instead of covering up and being like someone else, you will take your light and ignite someone else's light. Your light will cause their light to shine because, as you shine, you encourage and inspire others to do the same. Then, and only then, will the path to your destiny begin.

Meditation:

"The soul always knows what to do to heal itself. The challenge is to silence the mind."

~ Caroline Myss

Reflection Questions:

1. What are some unique traits about you?

_____

_____

_____

_____

2. Think about a time when you were emotionally wounded. How did it make you feel? Have you been healed?

_____

_____

_____

_____

3. What ways do you release things that have come to hurt you?

_____

_____

_____

_____

Chapter Eight

Embracing Change

"Be the change that you wish to see in the world."
~ Mahatma Gandhi

Everything in our lives will come to pass – there is nothing as permanent as change. Everything changes. Change is continual. We never arrive. We should always keep changing. There are 4 types of changes we experience:

1. **Change that happens to us** – change that comes with nothing necessarily to do with you. Example: a job layoff because the economy is bad (unexpected change) or a new baby/marriage (anticipated change)

2. **Change that happens around us** – our society, nation or even the world around us is changing. Things that used to be are no longer the same.

3. **Change that happens within us** – change that happens within us can affect us either

positively or negatively. It can affect us physically, emotionally, mentally or spiritually. Change that happens within us can come about because of something that affected us within.

4. **Change we initiate** – something created by plans we have implemented – deliberate change we set for the better.

We must learn how to embrace change. Embrace means *to take or receive gladly or eagerly; accept willingly. Many of us* DO NOT LIKE TO CHANGE. We fight change. We are married now but still want to do what we did when we were unmarried. We are mothers now and still want to do what we did when we were without children. We are adults now and still want to act irresponsibly. We are good with what we have, even if we don't particularly like it. This thinking keeps us living beneath God's best. Pride, fear, rebellion, laziness, stubbornness and so many others keep us stuck in a place of perceived comfort. If we do not change, we will not grow. We will die on the vine. God's desire is that we are changed into His image.

Change is not a new concept, and it has always been a difficult topic to experience. Ask Ruth and Naomi from biblical times *(Ruth*

1). Naomi was Ruth's mother-in-law. Within a couple of months, Naomi lost her husband AND her two sons. How do you adjust to life without someone that has been by your side for so long? It isn't easy, but it is also not impossible. Ruth could have given up entirely on Naomi and left her to fend for herself. However, she stayed. Ruth shifted her priorities and changed to make sure Naomi was cared for. They had to move to a new location, take up new jobs, and endure new difficulties. Still, they embraced change instead of running away or cowering behind the deaths of their spouse and family members.

Lasting change begins with renewing our minds. True change comes when we reprogram our minds with the Word of God. You and I can decide to change. Until we submit to the Word, do the Word, and live the Word; however, the change we think we're making will only be a temporary solution. When we change our thoughts, we change our behavior. That is true change. It is the Word that does the cutting. It is the Word that breaks through the flesh, the doubt, the insecurity, and the issues of life that hold us back.

To embrace change, we must develop an

intimate, personal and consistent relationship with the One who does not change. Intimate denotes closeness. When you have an intimate friend, they know things about you that no one else does. God desires to know us personally and for us to know Him. I must stay in the presence of the Father; in His presence is fullness of joy, peace, wisdom, knowledge, and understanding. We can either be changed by being in His presence or by the pressure of doing things outside of His presence.

We often fear change and will not embrace it because the fear of the unknown takes us out of our comfort zone. I know what this is, but if I change, what will it be? The right motivation will cause us to do things even if they are uncomfortable. Embracing change will keep us moving forward and focused on God and His Will for our lives. Embracing change will release potential. Potential is hidden, untapped power or dormant ability. Many people don't know what their potential is because they do not tap into it. It's there but dormant. When we embrace change, it can be a real benefit to us because we can realize there was more in us than we thought. We will experience greater personal success and fulfillment with little or no regrets. Embracing change will increase your faith and build up your strength in the Word.

Meditation:

"I am the greatest, I said that even before I knew I was."

~ Muhammad Ali

Reflection Questions:

1. How has your life changed in the last 90 days?

_____

_____

_____

_____

2. Would you say you embrace change or resist change?

_____

_____

_____

_____

3. What is the hardest thing about change to you?

_____

_____

_____

_____

Chapter Nine

Thank God I Don't Look Like What I Been Through

More than that, we rejoice in our sufferings, knowing that suffering produces endurance, and endurance produces character, and character produces hope, and hope does not put us to shame, because God's love has been poured into our hearts through the Holy Spirit who has been given to us. Romans 5: 3-5

During the process of change, there will be "those days." You know...those days where you wonder, "Why bother?" or "Why get up and get cute?" Those days when you want to lounge around in your favorite yoga pants while eating your favorite ice cream. Those days will happen, and in those days you must challenge yourself to "sparkle and shine." This means to exude the light and positivity within you despite the negative emotions you feel. On those days you will learn more about HIS plan for you. It is also on those days that the changes will be the most valuable. This chapter will help you figure out how to combat the negativity and focus more on your "sparkle and shine" this world deserves.

Change always starts in your mind. The way you think determines the way you feel, and the way you feel influences the way you act." - Rick Warren

STOP and Think: How do YOU define "sparkle and shine"?

If you are having one of the "those days," it is probably because of some type of problem. The good news is that every problem that exists in this earth already has an answer, thanks to God. No answer comes the same way through the same people; however, YOU (yes, you) are an answer to someone's problem. You have a purpose, and it is beyond just having material wealth and good. When you focus on the earthly issues (laundry, dishes, misbehaving children, etc.), you miss out on finding your purpose that helps you "sparkle and shine.

STOP and Think: What do you think is God's purpose for you so you can "sparkle and shine"?

Queen Esther (Esther 1), like you, had days when she didn't want to be who God created her to be. This was especially true when she ended up winning a contest and becoming the new queen of a nation. After becoming the new queen, she had an opportunity to do some good for her people. She could take a risk to make sure others like her wouldn't die because of the emotional outburst of a nobleman. Esther risked death to save other Jews like her, despite her emotions and saved thousands of lives.

Like Esther, you have a light with the power to help you AND others if you allow it to. And, these days, it is needed. Society has made criticism and negativity a powerful force to divide women among themselves. It is like there is some invisible competition going on that is unnecessary. If we all have our own "sparkle and shine," there is no need to compete. No need to curse. No need to be mean. We can all shine together. Plus, together you all have the power to inspire others.

STOP and Think: Who is someone you know that can help you "sparkle and shine"? Why did you choose that person?

Getting to your "sparkle and shine" may be a struggle like it was for me as I was moving through different phases of my life especially leading in church. I had to endure "those days" when I questioned the authenticity of my "sparkle and shine." Then, I had to encounter people who did not like the person I was becoming in Jesus. It was challenging to say the least as I was leading and I still had a husband and children to care for. It was...well...a lot. But, I took heed of my grandmother's words: "Tonya...Get up. Wash your face. Put on your make up. Get dressed. You don't have to look like your struggle." She was right. The art of "sparkle and shine" is not to "fake it until you make it." Instead, you rely on the greatness God has instilled in you to power through the valleys and heartache. You *faith* it until you make it.

Once you realize the "sparkle and shine" you have, how do you maintain it? Here are some steps you may want to consider:

1. **Value your "sparkle and shine."**

When it has value, you do not want to hide it. Remember, there is no need for comparison. There is no need to think you are unworthy. God created it especially for you. YOU!

2. **Do not hold on to things that diminish**

your "sparkle and shine."

Yes, we are nurturers and life-givers. However, we sometimes nurture and give life to things sucking us dry. Sometimes, it's people. Sometimes, it's us. Grudges. Gossip. Lust. Greed. Bitterness. I could go on and on. This is why it is important to keep moving toward the light even on "those days." The light heals. It delivers. It recharges you.

3. Let broken moments help your "sparkle and shine" and not hinder it.

The more broken you are, the more you surrender to God. The more you surrender to God, the brighter you shine. Sometimes, God allows us to sit in darkness so we can depend on Him as the light. Think of it this way. If a beautiful crystal cup falls to the floor, it falls to pieces. However, if light shines on them, they become glorious pieces of art. It's ok if you have moments when things are not perfect or not working in your favor. Those are perfect moments to make your "sparkle and shine" brighter and brilliant.

Meditation:

"If it is to be, it is up to me."

~ William H. Johnsen

Reflection:

1. Can you think of an example when your light shined the brightest?

_____

_____

_____

_____

2. Can you think of an example when you dimmed your light?

_____

_____

_____

_____

3. What can help you remember your light when all seems lost?

_____

_____

_____

_____

Chapter Ten

Why Me, Why Now?

"For many are called, but few are chosen."
Matthew 22:14 (ESV)

Sometimes, life can just make you wonder. We can go from a great moment to a low moment in a matter of what feels like split seconds. Then, we can believe that our low moment has never ended. Elijah knew this all too well. (1 Kings 19:1-4) Elijah was a prophet chosen by God to help King Ahab and Queen Jezebel understand how powerful God truly is. Elijah went toe to toe with the royalty's god, and Elijah won. This made King Ahab run home and tell his wife everything that happened. She was not really happy about that and vowed to kill Elijah as a form of revenge. When Elijah found out, he ran and ended up in the wilderness and asked God to *"Take my life, for I am no better than my ancestors who have already died."* (v.4)

I could understand his pain. Elijah has

just finished a major victory, and he is now running from an evil woman named Jezebel. He went from defeating 450 prophets of Baal as a bold, courageous, and victorious worshipper of God to running in fear because of one woman. He is now timid, fearful, and intimidated. He is exhausted from running, discouraged, and praying that he would die. How do you go from "It won't rain until I say it will" to "God, just take me now"? He went from an extreme high to an extreme low. Have you ever experienced it? God did just what He said. He blew your mind! You were so excited about what the Lord did! Then, something comes up to test your confession. I know that's happened to me, and I found myself asking 2 questions that I believe Elijah was asking, "Why me? Why now?"

Why me?

It may seem like the world is spinning out of control and circumstances keep changing day by day. That brings anxiety, stress, fear and frustration a lot like Elijah felt. I believe, however, a better question to ask is *what* instead of *why*. Usually, the questions of "why me" and "why now" come up most often when things are not going well, when we are under pressure, when things have shifted in a direction we are not comfortable with, or when things don't look like what we planned or even what we imagined. When we ask these questions, we get to a place where we have lost our peace. Sometimes, it even affects our will to move forward with hope.

"I know God will not give me anything I can't handle. I just wish that He didn't trust me so much." Mother Teresa

The *who* and the *what* must be more important to me than the *why*. The *Who* (Jesus) and the *What* (His Word) must be more important to us than the *Why*. The Word must guide us through this process. We can ask the questions. The challenge is to ensure we answer in alignment with the *Who* and the *What*. If we ask *What*, the answer is more definite, which helps increase our faith in God's abilities.

Believers are called to live by Faith and not by Feelings. When we live by faith, we live by what the Word says. The Word must be our guide, not our feelings. Our feelings must surrender to the Word. If we ask "Why", we are looking for an explanation. We want the explanation to please our emotions. Don't misunderstand. Your emotions are valid, and they have a purpose. But, emotions change and they are not stable. Maintaining faith is more consistent and dependable. One thing I've discovered about my walk with the Lord- faith pleases Him. Man says, "Show me and I'll trust you." God says, "Trust me and I'll show you."

Sometimes, we must follow Jesus without full understanding. Here is a reality for you: His ways are higher than our ways. We need to have His mind because He created us. There are things we won't fully understand with our natural minds. We just have to trust the Word. He is God and we are not. Some things we may not understand until we get to heaven. Can you be at peace with that? Things He will show us when we can handle it.

Change your confession from asking "Why Me" to thanking God it is you. Instead of saying "Poor me," declare "I can handle this because God is with me and He is for me." Instead of speaking your feelings, speak faith. Say what the Word says and change your perspective. When you change your perspective, even though you're walking through difficult times, you can still praise God because you know this is exactly where you are to be. He placed you right where you are now, agree with Him and live the life He intended for you.

Through my walk with the Lord, God gave me a Beatitude just for me: *"Blessed are the flexible for when they bend they will not break."* I have learned to truly live and move and have by being in Him. In this world, things will come to challenge you, frustrate you, irritate you, and discourage you. Yet, we can still be of good cheer. I have learned to make my plans, but I submit them to the Lord and trust Him with the results so I may not only survive but thrive. It's ok to not be ok. It's ok to ask why me if you answer the question according to What the Who says!

Why Now?

I also struggled with this question. It seems like sometimes God is unaware of the timing of things. Have you ever felt that way? Like this is just the wrong time for this. I can assure you, God knows exactly what He's doing.

God's timing is always perfect, even if it does not align with our timing. Sometimes, it can appear that God has forgotten or is showing up late. Sometimes, things will look like they are getting worse before they get better. When these moments occur, I believe it is purposefully to allow us to know that He is in charge, not us. His timing is divine. He shows up at the right moment. He sees the big picture. He already knows the goal and will accomplish the goal in His timing and His way. We must, by faith, trust He will show up ON TIME, not early, not late, but ON TIME – The exact moment.

We cannot speed up God's timing; however, we can slow it down. We can slow down God's timing or miss God's plan for our lives because of disobedience, impatience, or taking matters into our own hands. The Children of Israel had an 11 - day journey that took 40 years. And even at 40 years, some did not even enter. They had been suffering as slaves in Egypt for about 400 years. God sends Moses to deliver them. After a series of plagues, Pharaoh lets them go and they are now headed to a land flowing with milk and honey as God told them.

After all the great things God did for them, they still complained, they still doubted, they still murmured, and they could not just receive the blessing. God's timing is perfect, yet something is required from us. That is obedience: waiting and discerning His Will and His way.

God's timing is always appropriate. It is up to us to wait with a good attitude and use the time He has set for us to grow, overcome, and mature. I don't want to delay my breakthrough. I don't want to prolong my trial. I don't want to repeat the test. Thank God He is a God of another chance. Because of grace, we have another chance, so no condemnation. The power of grace will help us when we receive it and walk in it.

"Why now?" deals with time. Besides changing time zones, we usually think all time is the same. Actually, it is not. There are two types: *Chronos* and *Kairos*. *Chronos* deals with the sequential passing of time. Every year, there is a July 4th. Every year, we celebrate our birthdays. We use our calendars and watches to monitor *Chronos* time. *Kairos* time deals with moments. *Kairos* time is about appointed moments, things happening when they are supposed to according to God's set time. Clocks and calendars do not constraint it. Faith and opportunity help it to thrive.

So which one should we live by? While *Chronos* time is a gift, *Kairos* time is how the beauty of God works. He allows moments to show us just how amazing He is. When Christ died on the cross that was a *Kairos* moment. It was the exact moment and time for man's redemption. When we have *Kairos* moments, it allows us to get a glimpse of how God works;

how heaven operates. *Kairos* time is not about past, present or future – it is based around significance. It's not about schedules, appointments, or dates. It's about significant moments in time. It's when God decides to invade our lives to create *Kairos* moments in a *Chronos* world. Discerning *Kairos* moments are part of hearing God's voice and discerning what He is saying. Discerning helps you decide in difficult times and helps you give teachable moments to your kids.

One of the most difficult tasks I have ever had to complete was to accept my call to preach the Gospel. When my husband pioneered the church, God placed in his heart to establish and Pastor, my focus was just to help him do what God called him to do. I had no intention of preaching myself. Yet the day we had our first service, he asked me to do a scripture lesson. I took a scripture and expounded on the scripture.

At the end of the service, my father in love (my husband's father) came up and shared a word of wisdom. He told us we were both called to be a ministry team, we were to partner together in ministry to fulfill God's plan. I heard what he said but was not sure that was my assignment. I was a wife, a manager on my job, a mom to a 2-year-old son and an 8-year-old daughter. A few months after the first service, I found out that I was pregnant again. I felt like my hands were full – the last thing I could see myself doing was preaching. Well, in my time with the Lord, He spoke a word that I will never forget. He said, "I have called you to preach the Gospel. I have called you to stand with your husband to feed and care for the people. The fullness of what I have called you to do will not manifest until your children are older."

Those words meant everything to me. I wanted to honor God, yet He knew my heart was also to raise my children. It's been over 20 years now, and God has been faithful to give me the strength, wisdom, and grace to not only preach the Gospel but to raise my children. My youngest son, the one whom I found out I was pregnant with in one of the most challenging times of my life, is 20 years old. We named him Jonathan, which means Gift of God. He was a gift we didn't ask for, but we certainly needed and are grateful for!

I had to stop focusing on "Why me" and "Why now" and just trust God. When we get frustrated and weary, we ask "Why me" and "Why now" instead of proclaiming due season will come. At the proper time, the harvest will come. Keep sowing. Remember that there's an appropriate seasonal time gap for development between sowing and reaping.

Charles Francis Adams, the 19th-century political figure and diplomat who was the son of President John Quincy Adams and grandson of President John Adams, kept a diary. One day he entered: "Went fishing with my son today—a day wasted." His son, Brooks Adams, also kept a diary, which is still in existence. On that same day, Brooks Adams made this entry: "Went fishing with my father—the most wonderful day of my life!" The father thought he was wasting his time while fishing with his son, but his son saw it as an investment of time. The only way to tell the difference between wasting and investing is to know one's ultimate purpose in life and to judge accordingly. How do you view your moments right now with Jesus as your Lord and Savior?

Meditation:

"Instead of giving myself reasons why I can't, I give myself reasons why I can."

~ Anonymous

Reflection Questions:

1. Have you ever asked God, why me? Why now? When was the last time you asked?

_____

_____

_____

2. After reading this chapter, do you have any insight as to Why me? Why now?

_____

_____

_____

3. Instead of *why*, are there any *what's* you can identify?

_____

_____

_____

Chapter Eleven

What's Next?

Not that I have already obtained this or am already perfect, but I press on to make it my own, because Christ Jesus has made me his own. Brothers, I do not consider that I have made it my own. But one thing I do: forgetting what lies behind and straining forward to what lies ahead, I press on toward the goal for the prize of the upward call of God in Christ Jesus. Philippians 3: 12-14

As long as we are alive on this earth, there is always a next, God has for us. Sometimes we have listened to the voice of the enemy, the voice of others, or even our own voice that tells us it's too late. We have made too many mistakes, we have missed our opportunity, and we have blown it. We believe we are too old that too much time has passed. I do not believe that is the case.

I heard this phrase from when I was younger. Ben Franklin said, "If you fail to plan, you are planning to fail." Things don't just magically get better. However, with a plan, we can make progress.

So how to move forward? How do I go from where I am to the next phase in my life?

"Don't dwell on what went wrong. Instead focus on what to do next. Spend your energies on moving forward toward finding the answer."

~Anonymous

First, I must know that the past is gone. I can't try to live in it. Let's have a moment of reality right now. We cannot undo anything that has been done. We cannot unsay anything that has been said. All we can do now is move forward to a new place.

Every day is a gift. How will you respond to the new gift you have? How will you respond to the new opportunities presented to you? When we leave the past, we must leave the bad and the good behind. Live in that moment and do not hold on to past moments. We can look back, but we must be present. I love being a mom to my children. I love nurturing them, helping them, and caring for them. The way I do that now differs from the way I used to do that.

My children are 29, 22 and 20. What does it look like for me as a mom still cutting up my 20-year old's food? It would look strange, plus he would hate it. I learned how to embrace this new season. I learned how to be grateful for the years I had a hands-on approach to the season of now where I walk alongside. What holds us back sometimes isn't the bad that happened to us. Sometimes it's the good. It's the victories, the good reports, and the accomplishments. It's so good we just don't want to move forward.

Second, I make everyday count. We must approach every day as a gift from the Lord. Life is precious and short. Death is certain. It is a gift you should focus on what you can do and not what you can't do. We are not called to do everything. We all have a different assignment, and I must be okay DOING ME. Be intentional with your time and your energy (physical and mental energy). God is intentional, and He wants us to be intentional.

God expects fruit from our lives every day. Become a partner with the Lord. You must be an active participant; you must do your part. I can't just sit back expecting God to do everything for me. He helps us not does for us. There are some things we can do to frustrate the grace. He has a part, but we also have a part. We must believe. We must speak. We must have works to go along with our faith. To move forward into the new, you must forget the former things. Do not dwell on the past. Dwelling on the past will not change it.

Last, I must train myself to see beyond the facts. Fact is the current state. Truth is the reality of a thing. Fact is what I see; Truth is what the Word declares. It was a fact that Lazarus died, but the truth is Jesus is the Resurrection and when the Resurrection showed up, Lazarus had to get up. I must see myself the way God sees me. You may feel like you are in the wilderness and there is no way out, but God's Word declares He will make a way out. He will give you water in the desert. With Him, all things are possible.

Woman, it's your time to move. It's time for you to continue to walk your journey out! If God be for you, who can be against you? No one! You've got this girl!

Meditation:

"There were many times when truth spoke to me, but I did not listen. Often it called to me, but I did not hear it. I was too busy listening to lies. Unfortunately, if you listen to lies long enough, when truth speaks you cannot hear or bear it."

~ Lisa Bevere

Reflection Questions:

1. After reading this book, how will you now make every day count?

_____

_____

_____

_____

2. What do you need to let go of from your past?

_____

_____

_____

_____

3. What truth is God speaking to you today?

_____

_____

_____

_____

4. What truths can you use from God's Word to replace the lies/facts that you are believing?

_____

_____

_____

_____

Get Connected With Author Tonya McGill on Social Media.

She is the Founder of a 501© 3 nonprofit. *She3 Foundation* which exists to empower, encourage, and equip women.

 @ She3 Foundation

 @ she3foundation

 @she3foundation

Woman On The Move